In a catalogue relating to an exhibition of my work in 1975, I expressed the ideas underlying my drawing and painting as "a feeling of continuous and unbounded extension in every direction—*landspace*," combined with "a conviction that the history and development of the prairies is integral with a love of the land". These directions still hold true, and they have sustained a body of work during the intervening years.

Over the last two years, another dimension has been added in relation to my continuing exploration of the meaning of space in relation to painting. It is the concept of mobility in space.

The perceptual experience and the central expression of space have been extended to include motion as a catalyst for new concepts and structures. At a time when this catalogue is being formulated for a retrospective exhibition, it is appropriate to note that this most recent probe is still at an early stage of development. My hope is that it will be perceived as part of a cycle of events where ends are always beginnings.

Yates

May, 1983

QUARTER SECTION NO. 23
1974
acrylic on canvas
92.0 x 195.0 cm

TOWARD LANDSPACE

Ring House Gallery
The University of Alberta
Edmonton, 1983

Published in conjunction with a retrospective
exhibition held at the Ring House Gallery in
August–September, 1983.

Funding for this catalogue was provided by the
Alberta Art Foundation.

Canadian Cataloguing in Publication Data

Yates, Norman, 1923—
    Norman Yates toward landspace

Bibliography: p.
ISBN: 0-88864-963-0

1. Yates, Norman, 1923—   I. Ring House
Gallery.   II. Title.
N6549.Y37A4 1983   709'.2'4   C83–091269-X

Editing: Laura Hargrave
Design: Virginia Penny
Photography: Lauren Dale Photography,
Edmonton—cover, frontispiece, p. 9, plates 13, 23,
25, 30, 31, 32; Hans Blohm, Ottawa—plate 8;
Norman Yates, Edmonton—plates 14, 15, 16, 17;
John D. Dean, Calgary—plate 26; Douglas Clark,
Edmonton—plates 27, 28, 29; James Dow, Edmonton—
plates 18, 22.
Typesetting: The Typeworks, Vancouver
Colour separations: BK Trade Colour Separations Ltd.,
Edmonton
Printing: Speedfast Color Press Ltd., Edmonton

Cover: *Landspace 65,* 1982/83
charcoal colour, pastel, graphite on paper
232.0 x 288.5 cm

CONTENTS

The Alberta Art Foundation is most delighted to be able to participate in this exciting project, the exhibition and documentation of the work by Norman Yates.

Professor Yates' contribution to the cultural development of Alberta has been unequalled in time and depth as indicated in Ms. Collinson's introduction to this catalogue. The Foundation also has a very close association with Professor Yates. Appointed to the Alberta Art Foundation Board in 1975, Professor Yates was Chairman of the Board from 1976–78. He was the chief organizer of the Alberta Art Foundation Overseas exhibition to Japan in 1979 which confirmed the interest of cultural exchange between Alberta and the Japanese Prefectures we visited.

We feel most fortunate that Professor Yates' work is represented in the collection of the Alberta Art Foundation and we are grateful for his constant support to the Foundation. We congratulate Ms. Collinson's and her co-workers' effort in organizing this project.

Dale M.Simmons

Chairman
Alberta Art Foundation

This exhibition and catalogue have been prepared in a spirit of celebration; a celebration that honours two of Alberta's important cultural institutions and the artist who, more than any other, links these two institutions together. The University of Alberta is now 75 years old and the Alberta Art Foundation celebrates its tenth anniversary in 1983. Norman Yates has been part of the University for nearly 30 of its 75 years and his contribution to the Art Foundation, from its earliest beginnings, has been fundamental to the success of this endeavour. In addition to his early advisory work, Norman Yates served on the Foundation's Board for several years and he was one of its most successful Chairmen.

Although there have been many problems over the years, these institutions represent much of what is best in the life of the people of Alberta and, between them, they exemplify the realization of many creative dreams. These dreams are the foundation on which the really important heritage of a community stands.

Norman Yates' creative life is bound inextricably to the natural environment and to the community in which he lives. In addition to his personal expression as a painter, he has been actively involved with writers in producing such publications as *Edge* and the *White Pelican*. These were periodicals that provided an outlet for many Canadian poets and creative prose writers. Norman Yates also designed several important stage designs for Edmonton productions. Among his most complex were those done in collaboration with Wilfred Watson. We hope that the inclusion of Wilfred Watson's poem, written for Norman especially for this catalogue, will underline graphically the creative empathy so important to their collaborative efforts. This type of empathy resulted in a creative excitement in Alberta, the ramifications of which are perhaps still not fully explored.

This regional activity was supported by the critic, publisher, and writer, George Melnyk. He documented the work of visual artists who were committed to a Western Canadian expression and, in the Nu-West Press, also published works by Western Canadian writers. Through his own writing, Melnyk interpreted the creative activity around him. His interview with Norman Yates presents the artist now in as direct and straightforward a manner as possible.

We hope that the nature of the strong links between the environment and creative expression, which is felt by many Alberta artists, will be made more apparent by this study of Norman Yates' works since Norman, himself, is so committed to this philosophy.

The Ring House Gallery is grateful both to the Alberta Art Foundation for its support of this exhibition and catalogue, and to the University of Alberta for its continued encouragement of our programmes.

Helen Collinson

Director
Ring House Gallery

An Interview with Norman Yates by George Melnyk

The following is an interview with Norman Yates conducted by George Melnyk in the fall of 1982. Mr. Melnyk has published several articles on the painter's work. He is presently Executive Director of the Confederation of Alberta Faculty Associations.

Melnyk: I would like to begin by asking you about the growth you've witnessed in the art scene at the U. of A. since you first arrived in the fifties.

Yates: It was in 1954 that I was invited to come to the University of Alberta in the capacity of a painter-instructor. H. G. Glyde, Jack Taylor and myself made up the whole of the art department. In those early days there were very few places to exhibit other than the old Edmonton Art Gallery, but things started to open up in the early sixties. The old Department of Fine Arts, which included music and drama, separated into three professional departments. The purpose was not only to equip people to be appreciators, teachers or professors, but also to offer the opportunity for education to people who wished to become artists. During the seventies, art students became more confident that there was a place in society for an artist.

Melnyk: You're now entering your fourth decade as an artist. What are some of the phases you've experienced during that time?

Yates: When I came out west, I worked more or less as a realistic painter. Then in the late fifties and early sixties, I became more and more interested in the whole idea of symbolism. In the early seventies, we bought some land out in the countryside, and for the first time, I sensed that a space on which I could walk around without hindrance was excellently suited to the notion of multiple-space drawings. Other things followed from that—things like colour, a sense of place, the discarding of perspective and the expansion

and release into different formats. This direction eventually evolved into single works in which occurred some of the dynamics of those spatial relationships. These latter pieces were the works that gradually became popular in relation to the buying public.

Melnyk: What has been your response to this popularity?

Yates: I found that, ultimately, commercial success was not very profitable in terms of going on with new exploration in the studio because the demand was for a certain kind of work that was selling well. Consequently, I was very happy when I had a chance recently to have a study leave from the University and engage in the creation of work that had nothing to do with selling or with popularizing myself.

Melnyk: What happened during that year?

Yates: I tried to wipe my mind clear of all the former aspects. In other words, I put myself into the rather vulnerable position of not knowing what my intentions were. I had only the notion to get into a different environment. We went to England, where we hired a small car and drove about. We were constantly on the move and it was that quality of mobility that I found to be a key factor in later development. An idea was beginning to 'gel' about the artist in motion. Initially, the sketches had a fixed viewpoint, but eventually there were so many that they finally came to represent a free association of visual memories. They became more and more a number of experiences jammed into one drawing, even though when you looked at it, it seemed to look like one place.

Melnyk: How did your experience as an artist in motion express itself in a new kind of art?

Yates: I began making drawings on separate pieces of

paper but I let them grow and relate to other drawings on other pieces of paper, laying them side-by-side. So instead of one boxed-in drawing, I found a way that made me feel easy about moving in different directions. As a result of these spatial drawings, which I added to freely, I got the concept of relating one series to another. In the process, parts of each drawing are left deliberately white to permit spatial connection both laterally and vertically. The surface and the actual physical quality of the paper play parts in this action. I have now reached the point where there is no format, that is, a framed piece. I'm at the stage where the spatial concept is no longer contained. It can grow in any direction, in any shape, and can govern itself according to my energy and the nature of the materials, or the nature of the space in which it is produced.

Melnyk: Does this sense of release from format, this limitlessness have any spiritual implications for you?

Yates: I feel very optimistic and, in a way, right with the world because the world is providing me with a sense of space which makes human difficulties and problems seem temporary. One gets the feeling that the dots squabbling with each other in this vast space will be accommodated. Even if they destroy one another, the space will go on and the cycle of everything will continue to move.

Melnyk: Isn't this the sense of eternity, eternal time, eternal space, of the parabolic thing that extends forever and ever? Doesn't that also have a frightening aspect?

Yates: It's really a hard thing to explain. Spiritually one senses that in the same way that light in a forest shifts and moves and is changing every second, so oneself is changing in response to those things. Philosophically,

Norman Yates in his studio, 1983.

that sense of cycle and change feels so natural that it's not at all frightening.

Yatesian spaces

how	1	does
white	2	the
motion	3	of
(like	4	painting
a	5	white
compel	6	noise)
the	7	motion
business	8	picture

9 of

life	1	into
temporal	2	the
constraint	3	of
is	4	eternity,

5 Norman

Yates'	1	question.
rises	2	red
green	3	drops
deploys	4	blue
yellow	5	rallies,
the	6	let
white	7	metaphysics
this	8	of

9 silent

question	1	become
white	2	the
questions	3	of
silent	4	this

5 metaphysics

Wilfred Watson

Edward Norman Yates was born 7 September 1923 in Calgary, Alberta. Soon after his birth his family, who had emigrated from England just after World War I, moved to Regina, which they made their permanent home.

Norman demonstrated his love of drawing as a young child and received encouragement to pursue his hobby at home. His favorite childhood present was a large newsprint scribbler and crayons or pencils. Later, while attending Scott Collegiate Institute, he drew cartoons for the school newspaper, an experience which he remembers as an encouragement that he "could actually use his drawing ability to some advantage."[1] However, although the Yates family encouraged his interest in art as a hobby, it was never considered to be useful training for a future career.

The most positive and powerful influence on Yates' future development as a painter, the western prairie, was freely available within a short walk of the Yates family home on the edge of Regina. In spite of the dried-out earth and drifting soil, he developed a love for the varied beauty of the land and sky.

Another strong impression that became an influence on his art was his concern for his fellow men, an understandable outcome of growing up in Saskatchewan during the development of its democratic socialism in the 1930s.[2] Yates believes that "those who were born into the great space of the West formulated a spirit of community as a matter of physical survival and social need."[3] He vividly remembers witnessing the Regina Riot of 1935 when he was twelve. "By accident, we drove right in the middle of a confrontation. It was July 1. I remember it as a very exciting day; one that had real power and a tremendous imprint."[4]

Upon finishing high school in 1941, Yates joined the RCAF. An aptitude test indicated an ability in electronics and he was sent to McGill University to begin training as a radar technician. In November of

1942, Yates was sent to England where he remained until the end of World War II. On his occasional plane flights, the view of the world from the air reminded him of his experiences on the prairies as a boy:

I was aware almost constantly of a feeling of claustrophobia in eastern Canada and England. The view outside the airplane always released me. I liked to get up and above the world, especially in England... so I could get the same view as I did on the prairies. The spatial effect of the prairies is the closest one can get to a limitless sense of space... It was a psychological release to fly.[5]

While in England, Yates briefly visited a few art colleges and joined some 'life' drawing classes that were arranged for Air Force personnel at a nearby art school. These experiences convinced him to become a painter on his return to Canada, a decision he made against the advice of everyone but his wife, Whynona, whom he had married in England during the war.

After the war, Yates took another aptitude test to qualify for the Department of Veterans' Affairs rehabilitation financing. The result of the test showed that he should become a commercial artist (there was no fine art category). When Yates returned to Canada, he attended the Ontario College of Art, then considered to be the best art school in Canada. He completed the first basic year of his commercial art program, then switched to fine arts, choosing painting as a 'major' and graphics as a 'minor.'

Norman Yates, 1951.

1 Personal interview with Norman Yates, 7 November 1980.

2 Personal interview with Norman Yates, 7 November 1980.

3 Norman Yates, "Filmwest in the West," *Artscanada*, 29, No. 169/170/171 (early Autumn, 1972), 90.

4 Personal interview with Norman Yates, 7 November 1980.

5 Ibid.

13

Prior to World War II, artistic activity in Toronto had centred around three groups: the continuation of the Group of Seven, known as the Canadian Group of Painters; the Ontario Society of Artists; and the old established Royal Canadian Academy. The members of these somewhat conservative groups were the ones who exhibited regularly.[1] However, after the war, with many young artists and art students returning home, the art scene in Toronto began to become increasingly more vigorous and exciting.

Yates attended the Ontario College of Art from 1947–1951. The three instructors there who, according to Yates, had the greatest influence on his student work, John Alfsen, Harley Parker, and Fred Hagen, all produced fairly realistic portrayals of everyday life and people combined with some distortion for expressive purposes. Yates admired Harley Parker and enjoyed having conversations on artistic and aesthetic matters with this "most dynamic and interesting person."[2] Yates took a course from Parker in which colour theory was introduced, stimulating the young painter's interest in colour as an important visual force.

Yates attended drawing classes given by John Alfsen, who believed in the importance of fine draughtsmanship as well as the importance of the actual mark on paper, unsubordinated to description. The belief that the touch on the paper is the "prime force in a drawing . . . and gives it its personality and quality"[3] became one of Yates' basic artistic tenets. He remembers Alfsen's sensitive drawings as being characterized by a "sensual use of material," while the marks made by the soft pencil were "full of the joy of life."[4]

I got from him a sort of élan, flamboyance, flair, putting down the touch here and there . . . I remember wanting to develop that directness of touch that was more than just observational skills, more than just a knowledge in your head of what the structure was. It

somehow magically came down as something quite different on the paper that was very personal, and I found that to be a fascinating possibility for drawing.[5]

Fred Hagen introduced Yates to printmaking and stage design as artistic forms. With Hagen, Yates enjoyed discussing the "responsibilities of being an artist and his moral relationship to society."[6] It was Hagen, along with Harley Parker, who instilled in Yates "a sense of confidence in my attempt to become an artist."[7]

Eric Freifield was another flamboyant drawing teacher at OCA. Tacking huge sheets of white paper to the wall, and attaching a piece of black charcoal to the end of a long stick, he would make "bold, rather sensitive drawings with a directness of touch" to the delight of his large class of students.[8] The power of scale and scale relationships, which is of special interest to Yates, was perhaps first drawn to his attention by Freifield's 'performances.'

In contrast to Freifield, a "quiet excitement and intensity of belief" characterized Jock MacDonald's personality.[9] Yates did not realize it at the time, but he received the beginnings of an admiration for spontaneous, non-objective art from MacDonald.

Later, out in the middle of a field with a spatial notion, unable to do anything but be non-objective because I was walking all around the canvas, I'd suddenly remember Jock MacDonald.[10]

Another instructor was G. Röling, a visiting artist from Holland, who taught at OCA during Yates' final year of study. Röling exhibited a "disciplined approach to painting," and believed that emotional forces, while important, had to be "controlled into a manifestation of the surface."[11] He impressed Yates with a painterly approach to colour, as opposed to Parker's

SELF PORTRAIT
1950
oil on canvas
60.3 x 60.1 cm
plate 1

psychological or perceptual approach, and instilled in the younger painter the importance of the purity of transparent glazes that would remain an integral part of his work.

Yates' peer group at OCA consisted of mature students who had a sense of purpose about their art. In response to what they felt was an elitist system of institutional or highly commercial galleries, they formed a radical, anti-establishment group satirically called The Cadillac Club. With youthful idealism, they hoped to bring art away from the elitist areas of the city, back to the common people. This idea of making art relate to the people gained strength during Yates' last two years of college and became the direction of his future artistic expression.

The Gate, circa 1950 (plate 2), was made in conjunction with a class taught by Hagen. He encouraged the students to become psychologically involved with an idea and to use formal relationships and distortions to express their idea dramatically. *The Gate* reflects Yates' attempt at a comment on the urban scene. Here horizontal and vertical lines predominate, while an arc formed by a street light illuminates two derelicts. The use of contrasting white and black adds drama to the work and also reinforces the symbolic content of the scene.

The broken, spiky gate separates the observer's pleasant surroundings in the park from the oppressive urban scene of the two derelicts. A gate or passageway from one space to another physically and psychologically remains an important concept for Yates in his work. Another continuing thread in Yates' artistic development is the careful manipulation of the view, as exemplified in *The Gate*. Yates' student works, like *The Gate* were often expressive figurative renditions reflecting the urban scene.

After graduating from OCA with first class honors, Yates found it difficult to develop his career as a professional artist for several reasons. The Cadillac Club had dispersed, school studio space was no longer available and the Department of Veterans' Affairs financial support had ended, all of which left him rather at loose ends. So, for 'lack of a better plan,' Yates travelled to England where he worked as a bookkeeper for about six months.[12] In the weeks before leaving England, he attended the Festival of Britain of 1951, where he was especially impressed by the dynamic spatial explorations suggested by the architectural exhibits.

Leaving England in 1951, Yates and his wife toured northern Europe on a tandem bicycle for about three months. He was impressed with the way in which van Gogh's and Daumier's drawings and paintings still related to those ordinary people he met and observed as he rode through the villages and countryside.

During this trip, the young artist saw many original paintings, including works by Rembrandt, van Gogh, Picasso, and the Impressionists. Standing before the actual works, he was most aware of their surface.

When you get up close, it's marked, the brush strokes are apparent and you get a real sensation that the painter was standing in the same position you often stand in, in front of your own paintings ... It was almost as if I could fulfill the role of being the painter.[13]

The young painter was also strongly aware of the tactile quality of the painted surface, especially when confronting work by van Gogh or the Impressionists. His awareness that European society treated art as a very important part of living strengthened his conviction that as a painter, he was "part of a stream that had meaning and strength."[14]

By the end of 1951, Yates was back in Toronto. Along with Art Simons, an OCA classmate, Yates

THE GATE
1950
lithograph
33.6 x 25.7 cm
plate 2

established a studio on Bloor Street in an old Victorian mansion that the two used on evenings and weekends. The two also founded the Laurentian School of Art, teaching classes at night and on weekends, and painting during the day when they were not busy with commercial assignments. At the same time, Yates taught art classes organized by the Art Gallery of Toronto Extension Program. He participated in the first "Young Contemporaries" show in 1950,[15] but had no opportunity to exhibit in established galleries. He and Simons showed their paintings in theatre lobbies or golf clubs, sometimes making a few sales. Yates exhibited some watercolour sketches related to his European travels in the Beaches Library in 1952. The fact that the show was favorably reviewed in the *Toronto Daily Star* was encouraging for the struggling young artist.[16]

In the same year, 1952, Yates produced *Girl Drying Her Hair* (plate 3), in which he expressed a new, purely painterly interest, possibly inspired by paintings seen in Europe. The use of non-descriptive colour, as opposed to local colour, is taken further than in previous works, while the muted palette shows his appreciation of Picasso's early rose and blue periods, as well as his awareness of the cubist works he had seen. Again, Yates explores the possibilites of contrasting opposites in composition, colour and light, but the detail is more simplified than in earlier works. Perhaps the most important aspect can be seen in his treatment of the ground which has become as important a force as the figure, leading to an overall patterning effect.

During the period between 1951 and 1954, Yates painted watercolour sketches 'on the spot' in his favorite Toronto haunts. *Merry-Go-Round,* circa 1954 (plate 4), depicts a Cabbagetown scene. While painterly concerns are still important, an expression of social comment, equally strong, is expressed in the distortion of forms. In an attempt to depict symbolically the

GIRL DRYING HER HAIR
1954
oil on canvas
82.5 x 61.0 cm
plate 3

predicament of the people through the formal aspects of the painting, Yates distorts the horizontals, verticals and diagonals of the observed scene by portraying the buildings oddly foreshortened from different perspective views. This depiction leads to a suggestion of movement around the young child. The happy *Merry-Go-Round* atmosphere that the title suggests is contrasted to the plight of the child caught in the cycle of poverty. One will see that the use of contrasts in composition, colour, and theme, so evident in *Merry-Go-Round*, remains an important artistic device in Yates' later work.

Meanwhile, according to the artist, the Toronto art scene was improving steadily during the early 1950s. By 1954 there was a feeling that new things were beginning to happen in Toronto. It was precisely at this time, however, that Yates left Toronto to live in Edmonton.

1 See J. Russell Harper, *Painting in Canada: A History,* (Toronto and Buffalo: University of Toronto Press, 1966), p. 354, and Dennis Reid, *A Concise History of Canadian Painting* (Toronto: Oxford University Press, 1973), p. 238.

2 Personal interview with Norman Yates, 7 November 1980.

3 Ibid.

4 Ibid.

5 Ibid.

6 Ibid.

7 Ibid.

8 Ibid.

9 Ibid.

10 Ibid.

11 Ibid.

12 Ibid.

13 Ibid.

14 Ibid.

15 Yates recounted that the "Young Contemporaries" exhibitions were started by a similar group of artists who felt stifled by the established galleries. Yates exhibited in the first show in 1950 which was then called the "O'Keefe's Art Awards."

16 Hugh Thomson, "Tandem Bike Artist Exhibits at Beaches," *Toronto Daily Star*, 11 November 1952, p.7.

MERRY-GO-ROUND
1954
watercolour on paper
42.2 x 56.9 cm
plate 4

In 1954, Yates accepted a position for one year as an art teacher with the Faculty of Education at the University of Alberta. Although the art scene in Edmonton was limited, Yates was excited by the sense that "something fresh was beginning to happen in Alberta."[1]

In his first year in Edmonton, Yates became involved with live theatre at the University of Alberta by painting the backdrop for a Faculty of Education skit. This experimental beginning led to designing sets and costumes over the next fifteen years. Through this activity in theatre he met playwright Wilfred Watson, with whom he developed a lasting professional relationship and personal friendship.[2]

At the end of his year in the Faculty of Education, Yates was asked to join J. B. Taylor in the Department of Fine Arts, headed by H. G. Glyde. In conjunction with their teaching responsibilities on campus, Yates and the other art professors took part in community education. These duties ranged from such diverse activities as acting as a Special Supervisor of Art in certain selected areas of the province for the provincial school system's summer program, to acting as art critic for the *Edmonton Journal*.

An early attempt by Yates to depict the austere Alberta winter is seen in *Winter Landscape*, 1958 (plate 5). It is more abstract than previous works, because the forms and ground are interrelated by means of a slight rectangular patterning of the surface. Here, Yates attempts to "allow the forms to expand and have energy that moves from their surfaces and into space."[3] Environmental detail is thus softened and simplified in the process. Yates felt this approach led to a much greater awareness by the viewer of the actual surface of the work. The addition of ink markings over the surface also reaffirms the surface of the canvas in contrast to the three-dimensional illusion of the work.

Two Figures in a Space, 1960 (plate 6), is a

WINTER LANDSCAPE
1958
ink and gouache on paper
44.8 x 62.6 cm
plate 5

classically balanced composition suggesting an enclosed, stage-like space in which the artist disposes the figures and planes in a geometric manner. In contrast to the illusionary perspective, the gestural quality of the pencil strokes overlapping drawn boundaries, restates the surface flatness of the paper. The use of blues and reds for optimum contrast complements the formal contrasts in the composition.

The illusion of reality offered by a stage play obviously intrigued Yates, and contrasting illusion and reality remains one of his interests. In *Two Figures in a Space,* one figure appears on stage in an illusionary role, while the other appears in a stage-like space off-stage. This illuminates the beginning of a struggle, evident for a number of years in Yates' art, between a symbolically devised human figure and its relationship to the abstraction of the rest of the canvas.

Between 1961 and 1965, Yates produced a series of pencil drawings called the *Allegoria Series,* (plates 7, 8, 9), in which his ideas of symbolism and description entered a new cycle with a political and sociological message. Many of these cartoon-like drawings appeared in the Edmonton-based *Edge* magazine between 1963 and 1967. *Edge,* an independent periodical edited by Henry Beissel between 1963 and 1969, was dedicated to publishing Canadian poets, authors, and painters with radical viewpoints. The *Allegoria Series* which satirizes the abuse of power in contemporary society, complemented many ideas expressed in *Edge.*

The gnome-like figures depicted are often satirizations of priests, court jesters, or kings, with the populace acting in 'mobs.' The works range from comical satire where the figures appear to be simply silly to more sobering depictions of cruelty. *Allegoria 3* (1963) exemplifies Yates' fine draughtsmanship, and is one of the few pencil drawings discussed in Arnold Rockman's "How 20 Canadians Draw the Line."[4] The composition consists of a dramatic movement with secondary circular forms that sweep the gnome-like creatures unthinkingly along. No intelligent individual actions are seen as they all join the noisy drummer in his cause.

Allegoria drawings relate to Yates' mature *Land Drawings* in the way that the 'mark' is applied to the surface of the paper, and the large amounts of white paper left untouched by the pencil.

In 1963, Yates spent a sabbatical year at the University of Durham in Newcastle-on-Tyne in England. Here he met British painter, Victor Pasmore, who was producing abstract relief constructions which were mathematically geometric and simple. He was also a pioneer in the English concept of a design orientation to schools of fine art and it was primarily this aspect of Pasmore's work that attracted Yates.[5] Pasmore was also designing housing units with architects in a team approach. Providing aesthetically good living quarters for ordinary people appealed to Yates' political and sociological ideas.

In England, Yates was aware of the strong sense of atmosphere and surface bathed in a soft light as he continued his personal triangular struggle between symbolism, objective rendering, and abstraction. *Landscape,* 1963 (plate 10), is an abstraction of the English countryside. The main compositional force is the diagonal road with the small cocoon-like area as the focal point. The feeling of small scale, closeness, and surface in England, inspired Yates to attempt an overall design, forcing objects to the surface. He further increases the surface quality using gestural slashes over the forms.

Durham Landscape, 1963 (plate 11), represents the other side of Yates' artistic struggle between abstraction, symbolism, and description. After forcing himself to explore many possibilities in his art, he would return to this type of rather traditional landscape painting for relaxation. This calm, descriptive rendering of the scene

TWO FIGURES IN A SPACE
1960
watercolour and pencil on paper
44.7 x 57.0 cm
plate 6

ALLEGORIA 12
1964
pencil on paper
48.3 x 61.0 cm
plate 7

ALLEGORIA 8
1961
blue pencil on paper
45.7 x 61.7 cm
plate 8

ALLEGORIA 14
1963
blue pencil on paper
48.4 x 61.0 cm
plate 9

LANDSCAPE
1963
gouache on paper
66.8 x 52.0 cm
plate 10

DURHAM LANDSCAPE
1963
watercolour and pencil on
paper
44.5 x 56.9 cm
plate 11

shows Yates' training and demonstrates his comfort with this approach to landscape. The influence of Pasmore is evident, however, since *Durham Landscape* is painted in a looser, more fluid manner than previous works such as *Winter Landscape*. In composing *Durham Landscape*, Yates used naturally occurring horizontals and verticals combined with subdued tones so that the pale English sun is slightly visible through the heavy air.

Yates spent the summer of 1965 at the University of British Columbia as a visiting professor. During that time, he seriously analyzed his work, acknowledging the several directions in which it was moving. Following this period of introspection, Yates attempted to reconcile all his ideas of description and abstraction, illusionary perspective and pictorial surface, satire and symbolism.

The experimental *Throne Room Series* consists of pencil drawings and paintings in acrylic, to which wood, metal foil, and found objects are added. The *Throne Room Series* was less realistic than the *Allegoria Series*, but continued the theme of 'abuse of power.' Yates freely added established symbols of power to his own 'personal mythology' of power symbols. In this excerpt from an article written for *Edge*, Yates discusses the thematic core of his work:

My aim is to play the symbol. The symbol is derived from the congestion of the imagemakers. There is, of course, more to the world than just the power struggle, but it happens that at this moment in time it is this that has caught my eye and my symbol.[6]

A simplified queen figure became one of Yates' central symbols of power at his time. *Queen Head*, 1965 (plate 12), is rendered in powerful, aggressive strokes which give rise to unpleasant tactile and visual sensations to indicate the queen's abuse of power.

QUEEN HEAD
1965
graphite on paper
61.0 x 45.5 cm
plate 12

Wall Painting I, 1968 (plate 14), is an interesting example of Yates' attempt to bring many ideas together. Perceived from a distance as an abstract field, closer observaton reveals a small area at the bottom containing rows of real toy soldiers. These are backed by illusionary soldiers rendered in perspective in bright colour. In this painting, Yates plays his favorite game, setting up contrasts and dynamic relationships. Not only do the surface-oriented areas, like the strip of wood, the metal circle, or the toy soldiers, produce contrasting tactile sensations, but they also contrast to the visual reference of the realistically rendered soldiers that recede into depth. The reality of the wooden strip also contrasts to the painted line, while the varied handling of paint and the contrast between hard and soft edges also produces various tactile and visual effects. Yates explains that once the viewer is captured by the painting, the "actual object, the painted illusion, the formal structure, and the symbol all combine to engage the viewer, to envelop his mind, and to invite reciprocity."[7]

In these works, Yates developed a symbolic vocabulary that strengthens as the viewer's conscious and subconscious associations with the symbols increase. The choice of symbols relating to British sovereignty likely stems from Britain's long history of power and imperialism as well as Yates' personal connections with that country. Linking the sovereignty symbol with war, which can be seen as the ultimate abuse of power, the artist creates a powerful, recurring theme typical of the 1960s when society in general questioned reality, illusion, and power.

COURTESAN
1965
graphite, watercolour, balsa
wood, black tape on paper
68.9 x 92.5 cm
plate 13

1 Personal interview with Norman Yates, 7 November 1980. Yates vividly recalls driving through heavy rains in Saskatchewan to clear skies in Alberta and watching the "landscape change from one of surfaces to one of space."

2 Wilfred Watson is a playwright and poet who taught at the University of Alberta for many years. During the time that Yates and Watson worked together, they shared an interest in the theories of Marshall McLuhan. Yates and Watson continue to exchange ideas about their work and share an interest in spatial concepts.

3 Ibid.

4 See Arnold Rockman, "How 20 Canadians Draw the Line," *Canadian Art,* No. 90 (March, April, 1964), 85-95.

5 Yates may also have been attracted to England because he had many emotional ties with that country. His parents and wife came from England. Yates was impressed with what he calls the liberal attitude of the English who gave him a job when he lived there in the early 1950s.

6 Norman Yates, "Metal Flags and Cloth Medals," *Edge,* no. 9 (Summer, 1969) p. 78. Yates' interest in contrast is evident in his choice of title.

7 Ibid.

WALL PAINTING I
1968
acrylic on canvas
101.2 x 101.2 cm
plate 14

KINETIC FOIL
1969
two rows of Alcan aluminum
foil
304.8(h) x 243.8(w) x
609.6 (d) cm
installation piece
plate 15

As the 1970s approached, Yates became increasingly involved with the artistic possibilities of various media such as photography, holography, and filming. Although he later abandoned these experiments, they advanced his understanding of spatial concepts and their application to the more traditional arts, drawing and painting.

As the city grew, the art scene changed. The Edmonton Art Gallery sponsored the "Air Art" and "Place and Process" exhibitions in 1969 which drew national and international attention. Yates' 1969 exhibition at the Students' Union Art Gallery on the University of Alberta campus was entitled "Extensions," a McLuhanesque term. However, Yates did not agree with McLuhan that the traditional arts belong to a vanished world. Yates stated that he wished to maintain "the rich medium of painting" but also create an expansion from its surface when required by creative interaction. He wanted to pursue "his art beyond the limits of the canvas."[1]

A discussion of one of the pieces in the exhibit, *Kinetic Foil,* 1969 (plate 15), will serve to illustrate Yates' interest in environmental art and spatial ideas. Once the viewer enters the corridor, he becomes part of the composition. The shiny silver foil interacts by reflection with the exhibition space and changes constantly as it is affected by changes in lighting, movement of the viewer, and even general traffic on the other side of the window beyond the work. The reflective quality brings other colours and forms into the constantly changing work as secondary composition elements.

The movement, sound, and reflection of *Kinetic Foil* extends past the formal aspects, to the theme of the work. The viewer participates when his reflection becomes part of the surface of the work. The work, itself, seems to take on life by its movement and sound at the same time as it stimulates the viewer to 'play'

with the piece. The theme of a human entering a new space and beginning a dynamic relationship with that space becomes an integral one in Yates' later *Landspace* works. With "Extensions," it is quite clear that spatial concepts have now come together in Yates' work with stage designs, paintings, and experiments in various media.

In 1969, Yates took part in an exciting experimental theatre event when he designed the sets and costumes for Wilfred Watson's *Let's Murder Clytemnestra According to the Principles of Marshall McLuhan* (plate 16). The play "suggested (to Yates) a new kind of design possibility, a shimmering, non-permanent, flexible space, four-dimensional and dynamic."[2] Because the play was expressionistic and symbolic, Yates felt free to experiment and gave the audience an electronically produced, multi-spatial view of the action.

Yates was familiar with Marshall McLuhan's idea of focusing on one thing to the detriment of the whole, and thought it would be interesting to let the audience have a full view of what was happening on all sides. A similar idea had been expressed by the cubists nearly sixty years earlier. However, with the art of electronic media, the idea of simultaneity could be applied in a new way to a stage play. The electronically produced, multi-spatial view made possible with cameras, sixteen monitors and a large telebeam screen was an exciting experiment in exploring the perception of space.

The result was sixteen (serial) images of the set. The red and blue glowing columns, combined with thin, horizontal, plastic strips framing the action, showed the audience images often missed in a stage play like the "off-side view, the intimate close-up, the hidden gesture, the glinting eye, the sensuous mouth or the suggestive action—a multi-image of the live action."[3] The extravagant set was perfectly reconciled with Marshall McLuhan's theories, but unfortunately confused the audience somewhat.

Set design for *Let's Murder Clytemnestra According to the Principles of Marshall McLuhan* by Wilfred Watson
1969
plate 16

For Yates, "scale is always fascinating and a face in sensitive expression some ten feet high and only twenty feet away can be quite powerful."[4] With his design for another Watson play, *Up Against the Wall Oedipus,* in 1970, Yates carried on his exploration of the effects of scale relationships. Filmed sequences of the play were related to live actors and projected on a huge screen at the back of the stage, which had a visual effect of dwarfing the live action. Yates was excited by his ability to manipulate the electronic media both visually and audibly so that the filmed sequences created the illusion of a large space from the reality of the relatively small space of the stage. The exploration of the various artistic uses of scale and focus begun in these stage designs became increasingly important to Yates in the 1970s.

From 1970 to 1972, Yates did not produce any paintings, but instead concentrated on photography and film making. He also organized, hosted, and did the cinematography for three educational programs for CTV, which gave him the opportunity to combine his ideas on education with his interest in the media of television.

In 1971, Yates joined the *White Pelican* magazine. This magazine, a quarterly review of the arts, was started by its general editor, Sheila Watson. Between 1971 and 1976, Yates co-edited one issue a year, usually with John Orrell.[5] His interest in the relationship between parts led him to make book-like collages of drawings or photographs related to sequence, seriality, and the development of an idea over time. In one self-portrait series done in 1971 for the *White Pelican,* titled *Self Portrait with 3M* (1972), Yates relates vertical bars to his physical self. These slowly disappear, finally leaving only a horizontal line across the centre of the page, expressing his ultimate death and union with land or nature.[6]

In retrospect, Yates now sees the 1960s as a period of

a second maturing. He found his work with various media, like filming, too physically demanding, and returned to the "purity of drawing and painting after all the excitement of experimentation."[7]

1 Norman Yates, "Extensions," December, 1969, from the artist's personal files.

2 Norman Yates, "Designing Clytemnestra," CKUA January 1970, p. 2, from the artist's personal files.

3 Ibid., p.3.

4 Ibid., p.5.

5 See "Norman Yates: Self-Portrait with 3M," *White Pelican*, 2, no. 2 (1972), 3–7.

6 Personal interview with Norman Yates, 12 December 1980.

7 Ibid.

island 1

2

3

4

THE ISLAND
black and white photographs
162.0 x 50.5 cm
plate 17

In *Unnamed Country*, Dick Harrison discusses the influence of culture on our reaction to the landscape. He argues that the first English-speaking people in the West, including artists, "looked out on the prairies with essentially 'Eastern' eyes. Their perceptions were so conditioned that in the most prosaic and literal sense, they could not see clearly what was around them."[1] Before the problem of how to paint the prairie comes the question of how to perceive the prairie.

In the early 1970s, Yates experienced a profound change in the style and subject of his art. Along with other Alberta painters, he attempted to disregard past traditions and to initiate in his work a fresh interpretation of his environment. His art began to reveal his perceptual, psychological, and cultural self to be rooted firmly in the prairie.

The focus on 'space' that became Yates' greatest pictorial interest in 1972 did not separate itself from his long time interest in humanity. In depicting the Regina Riot of 1935, Yates combined a historical event that became a symbol with a distinct personal memory from his own past, which took him back to a time and an issue that he felt was important to himself and to prairie people in general. Yates, in his depiction of this riot, begins to explore the possibilites of solving the spatial dilemma of the open prairie in a new way.

In forming *Two Space Regina Riot 1935,* 1972 (plate 18), Yates joined two pieces of paper together laterally. With this totally horizontal basic component, he understood for the first time the power of the oriental format which leads to the portrayal of frontal, surface space. Within the perimeter set for himself, he felt that he could use a western illusion of depth and still maintain the surface in his mind. While the division between the two pieces of paper acts as surface-maintaining device, Yates visually perceived the surface of the white paper surrounding the division as space. For the first time, he realized that the physical quality of the surface of the paper could be equated with space, and any added 'marks' would have to relate either to the surface of the paper or to illusionary depth, and, if possible, to both.

The paradox between attempting to express limitless space on a two-dimensional surface, which had bothered him for some time, began to resolve itself in the artist's mind. He began to see the problem more as the dialectic of two attitudes toward perceiving and portraying space. The two poles could relate and enhance each other almost in an oriental sense, and not confront each other as two opposites in the western sense. Yates expresses his view of the dialectical nature of the world which he had formed slowly over the years.

I tend to see the world . . . as a series of relationships with differences. Dualities may occur and there may be opposites occurring but they're always dynamic. Night and day are not opposites, but they are transitional things that occur. They move through a space where the relationships are sometimes very close and sometimes quite far apart. Relationships are stronger than opposites. The relationships start from the point where one happens to be located and that's what I sense to be a dynamic force.[2]

In keeping with his philosophy of the nature of visual relationships in the world, Yates attempts to have the diverse visual components of his work relate as well. In this drawing, *Two Space Regina Riot*, a concentration of light and dark areas reinforces the visual power of each area. In the centre of the work one finds a large area of pure white paper. This area appears bathed in the "harsh, brilliant, big, bright light" of the prairie.[3] Where the pieces of paper meet on the surface, there are pressures and tensions. These pressures expand laterally toward the contrasting darks which are grouped toward the outer edges.

Yates extends his idea of the duality of nature to the marks that he adds to the white surface as well. The simple, economical lines which describe figurative elements like a person or a car also perform "abstractly on the surface and into space as a line."[4] Although the large size of the cars indicates their position in the foreground of the scene, the large amount of white paper within the lines makes the cars appear to sink back into the distance away from the pictorial surface. On the other hand, the small, sharp silhouette of a figure can, at times, appear to move up to the surface as it catches our immediate attention, having as strong a focal point as the much larger cars. Because of the strength of the small area of concentrated black, the silhouetted figure can also be perceived as a 'hole' or opening in the surface. On the other hand, because of its small size, the figure can appear as an object in the far distance in the sense of the scale relationships in western perspective. This spatial dichotomy consisting of a dynamic interplay between the observer's perception of surface and depth as opposed to a drawing based upon a mathematical perspective system, where all horizontal lines come together in a vanishing point on the horizon, characterizes the illusive quality of space which Yates attempts to capture in the fixed format of a drawing. This broad concept became a focus for him during the years of 1972 to 1974, and continues into the present time.

With this drawing of the Regina Riot, Yates has combined form and content to create "the unity of the western landscape with western history . . . Though the historical setting is urban, the prairie landscape is there in its overpowering horizontal presence, in the black and white bleakness of the depression and fruitless land."[5]

Jim Simpson, writing for the *Edmonton Journal*, has observed that the drawings of the *Regina Riot Series*

43

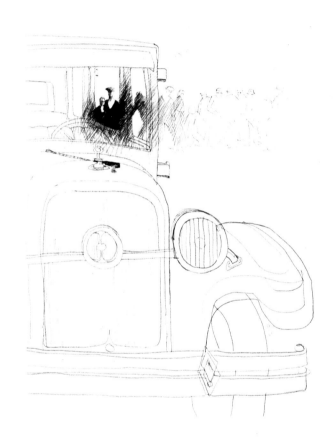

TWO SPACE REGINA
RIOT 1935
1972
graphite pencil on paper
66.0 x 202.4 cm
plate 18

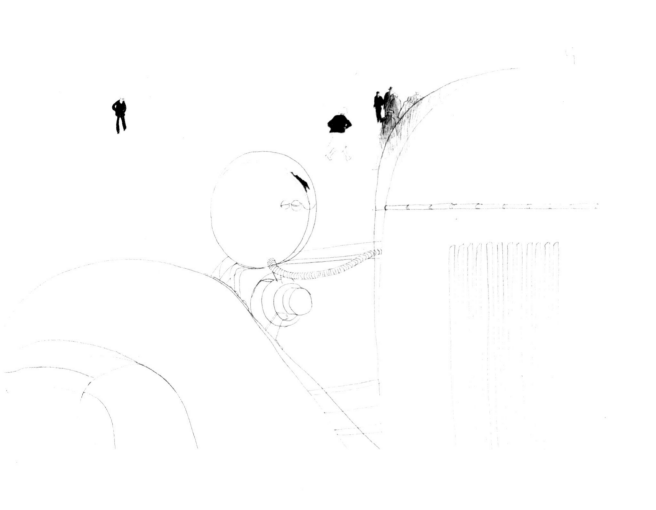

"bear witness to some aspects of perception and memory that were revealed to Yates in his study of photography–filmmaking in particular." They show his knowledge of "multiple image, sequence, and flashback."[6] This relationship is not surprising when we remember that Yates began his 'focus' on space while looking through the lens of a movie camera. At the same time, Yates relies to a great extent on his memory in creating these images since they relate to his mental image retained from that moment, years ago, when he saw the Regina Riot in progress. This aspect adds to the film-like quality as his visual memory of the event consists of a view through the window of a car which would have cropped the action indiscriminately, like a camera. Finally, Yates supplemented his own memory with black-and-white photographs of the actual riot for visual references. Thus, with the *Regina Riot Series,* Yates combines a personal memory, documented history, and creative imagination to arrive at his final statement on paper. The documentary quality of the series is enhanced by the quality of the drawn lines, since Yates allows the process of applying the 'mark on the surface' to remain on the paper.

In this series, Yates portrays a mob as he did in the *Allegoria Series,* but this time the mob is victim of a larger power and in conflict with that power. One individual, however, stands out by action, colour, and compositional importance in the central panel. In his careful fusion of form and content, Yates portrays this lonely individual as he strikes out against impossible odds.[7]

In 1972, Yates took part in a group exhibition called "For an Independent Hairy Hill" in which some Alberta artists decided to make a statement affirming that their local roots were worthy of artistic inspiration.

In an essay titled "From the People - From the Land - The Art of Norman Yates," George Melnyk, a spokesperson for prairie writers, poets, and painters, states that Yates' art "reflects the struggle of being an artist in the West, of creating on the periphery of contemporary art movements rather than at its centre."[8]

He goes on to argue that the land has been the most important factor in the western identity, stating "the only barrier that has stood in the way of having the western self totally defined or absorbed by the (East) has been the land."[9] In this same spirit of cultural awareness, Norman Yates later acknowledged his close feeling for the land:

Western history and western landscape are bound inextricably. The land is part and parcel of our history and our history has to do absolutely with the land. For me, the land is our basic metaphor.[10]

In the early 1970s, while Alberta was rapidly emerging as a confident, powerful province, Yates voiced the new confidence felt by many Alberta artists that made the Hairy Hill show possible:

The Alberta artist should not feel at any disadvantage because he is not living in Toronto. He may not get the international recognition that a Toronto or New York artist has access to by virtue of location but he is capable of the same art. A narrow regionalism is just no longer possible.... Art, good art, is being made at a lot of odd and out of the way places now. London, New York and Paris are not the ultimate source of aesthetic influence.[11]

Interest in the vital new art scene in Alberta and in the prairie provinces in general, spread to other parts of Canada and enough excitement was generated to warrant the autumn, 1972 edition of *Artscanada* with its theme "Prairie Spaces and Places."[12]

Parallel to the general revitalization of the Alberta art scene, Yates sees his involvement in the Hairy Hill

*DRAWING 2, REGINA
RIOT 1935*
1972
graphite pencil on paper
66.0 x 101.2 cm
plate 19

exhibition as a personal artistic milestone. Participation in the exhibition forced him to bring his ideas together once more as he had in the summer of 1965, but now there was a solid focus to his art. For Yates, "the beginning of the 1970s was as if someone opened a door."[13]

Four Space Elevator with Brand, 1972 (plate 21), which appears on the Hairy Hill exhibition catalogue cover, marks a significant turning point in Yates' oeuvre: his return to the purity and tradition of drawing. The prairie grain elevator is a traditional western image and landscape painters have for years been inspired by its vertical form in contrast to the empty prairie. Here, however, Yates gives the mundane subject new life. The elevator has been recreated as a large vertical monument expanding over the four sheets of paper which are arranged vertically with a small margin between each sheet of paper. These horizontal breaks between the sections restate the literal surface of the format of the pieces of paper as they add a horizontal element to the total composition.

Formally, this drawing explores the concept of 'focus,' an idea which occurred to Yates when he was in the country filmmaking. The drawing was composed later once the idea had distilled in his mind. He realized that if he were close enough to get the detailed character of the elevator, the texture and colour of the peeling, broken boards, he would lose the whole image; and if he were distant enough to capture the whole, he would lose the particular details. So he attempted to convey the concept of focus as a useful, expressive device.

Yates drew parts of the landscape and elevator on large pieces of paper at a fairly short distance from his subject and then attached the 'modules' together. The resulting image of the elevator is ten feet tall, and in spite of its size it retains a great deal of detail. The seemingly simple idea of retaining two focuses, one of surface detail or description and the other of the gestalt

or whole, in the same two-dimensional space excited Yates, who felt that he was coming closer to understanding spatial relationships. Another characteristic of the drawing, of which Yates was aware, was that separately each piece of paper formed an abstract drawing and if that concept were pursued, each detailed, descriptive work, depending on 'focus' might appear as a non-figurative image.

Because Yates was experimenting with 'focus', he reduced his colour to a black-and-white range in order to concentrate on the main issue. The use of black and white is related to photography and filmmaking and gives a general documentary character to the drawing.

In contrast to the large size of the work, the politically oriented symbolism is carried by a fairly small area. Instead of the name of a small prairie town, as is sometimes seen on a grain elevator, a corporate symbol appears alone. Yates implies in this manner that the typical prairie image which westerners see as their own is owned and controlled by a distant corporation.

While Yates' work during the early 1970s became increasingly personal due to his perceptual search, with an attendant search back to his own historical 'roots' in the prairie, another personal force exerted itself. In 1972, Yates acquired what he has come to call his Land Studio, a quarter section of land sixty miles west of Edmonton, "rich in the line, the texture, and the contours which comprise the Alberta landscape."[14] Yates now believes that his rediscovery of 'the land' revitalized his career:

I have a conviction that the history and development of the prairies is integral with a love for the land. We discard that love and we lose our soul. My drawings and paintings are based on the landscape and the people I find there.[15]

With his new, close relationship to the land, Yates'

THREE SPACE REGINA RIOT 1935
1972
graphite pencil on paper
198.2 x 101.6 cm
plate 20

perceptions of the world entered his work as never before. Edmund Husserl, founder of phenomenology, referred to "the immediacy of perception." That is, when a person finds himself in a crisis, or simply a new situation or environment, he becomes acutely aware of his own personal perceptions and uses these perceptions to interpret the world.[16] So, as Norman Yates began to paint the landscape of his new Land Studio, he attempted to relate his own personal perceptions to the artistic tenets with which he was so familiar.

Maurice Merleau-Ponty, another famed phenomenologist, defined perception as a sensory-motor behaviour, through which the world is "constituted for man as the world of human consciousness prior to any explicit or reflexive thought about it."[17]

As an artist, Yates is very aware of the importance of his perceptions of the world. He believes that a "chief barrier to communication is simply a matter of language," while "people, no matter where they are, relate to the same spatial context," or share common perceptions of the space surrounding their bodies.[18] He further explains his awareness of the space around him:

The thing that I describe as a spatial relationship universally is certainly one I feel in everyday occurrences with people or with objects. I didn't deal with that notion in earlier times. I was always looking symbolically through a window before. Now the relationships are much closer, in some ways more disturbing. But they are more energetic, certainly.[19]

Yates believes that as an artist, he is only able to "partially understand the visual phenomena, translate it through myself, and manifest it in paintings and drawings."[20] Yates agrees that personal perceptions become universal by virtue of the common fact that we all share our humanness.

Of course, we do not exist simply in the 'real' world of perception. There are many levels of experience, and Yates is aware of the complexities of reality that start with perception:

The reality of objective consciousness, I believe, must be regarded as only the 'outer skin' of reality, and that mainly through a non-intellectual imaginative capacity to experience will a truly rich grasp of oneself as a person in relation to other persons and to one's environment come about. In whatever I try to do, my attitude and feelings are shaped I think by my awareness of others, by my need to somehow reach them and by the need of my reactions to respond to them.[21]

Jean Paul Lemieux, a Quebec painter, inspired Yates with his depiction of space, and indeed, they share many common influences and attitudes. Both painters found that a change in their environment reinvigorated their perceptions of the world around them and led to a profound change in their art at a relatively mature age. They also share a fairly sudden sense of confidence in the value of painting their own world inspired by their own perceptions. Finally, they both receive their artistic inspiration from the spacious quality of the Canadian landscape. Lemieux's awareness of this spaciousness came during a journey by train when he "was struck...by a strange spatial quality about the landscape."[22] Yates, on the other hand, attributes his awareness of the spaciousness of Alberta to his experiences on his Land Studio: "My experience on the land gives me more of a notion of space, a vision of an expanse of country combined with a feeling of continuous and unbounded extension in every direction."[23]

With *Two Space Quarter Section #20,* 1973 (plate

50

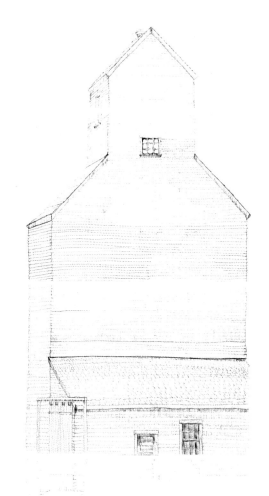

FOUR SPACE ELEVATOR
WITH BRAND
1972
graphite pencil on paper
304.8 x 104.5 cm
plate 21

23), Yates has combined formalist elements typical of modernist concerns with an attempt to portray the essence of the Alberta landscape. In order to translate his perceptions onto the pictorial surface, to flow visually through the surface, the painter combines an illusion of space with an emphasis on surface handling. Many opposites are utilized: horizontal and vertical areas, hard edges and soft edges, light and dark colour. In this light-filled painting, time becomes part of space or the universe, and its relative permanence contrasts with our limited time and space as mortals living on the earth. Yates has removed the human figure from the canvas, and now the human element consists of the observer standing temporarily in front of the painting.

With his work in 1972, Yates joins the developing prairie tradition of attempting to capture the intense light, raw colour, and vast space of the prairie. The paintings are perceptual in their inspiration stemming from the prairie and conceptual in the transformation of this prairie space into the surface of the canvas. These works by Yates are firmly based on his exploration of the visual phenomena of the Land Studio and go beyond a mere description of the visual phenomena, as they reach out to encompass the perceptual phenomena of light, space, and time experienced by mankind.

Thus, one finds that with these landscapes, Yates has carried on his idea initiated in the "Extensions" exhibition in 1969 where he explored the concept of expanding his work by leaving the "fixed and permanent" and moving toward a flexible non-permanent space as he constantly attempts to come to grips with his awareness of a continually changing image of reality. The painter discovered that simplification was a key to the dilemma:

(A) distinctive feature of life in Alberta, related to the nature of the land and its effects on the people, is the consciousness of space. Volume, compression, and corridor seem to me to be characteristic of large city living, but in the West, people are still peculiarly aware of the openness of the sky and the spread of the land.[24]

Although, in the above words, Yates is discussing film, he could just as easily be referring to his own drawings and paintings. This awareness of space has caused Yates to become more conscious of time and detail. Because he is not bombarded with too much detail in a small space, he sees more, and has the time to study what he sees carefully, to allow his perceptions to savour the image before him. He is aware of the elusive nature of prairie space and attempts to capture this quality that one can come close to, but never reach:

The spatial interest is curious because it really has to do with something that isn't there and conceptually it's hard to make it solid. Philosophically, it's really energetic, a dynamic thing that we'd normally associate with either the impact of solids or the splitting of solids. We never associate it with what happens at a distance between solids, and that is psychologically hard to do until you realize that most of our lives, we're walking along roads, through corridors, between objects . . . it becomes obvious that perhaps the spatial aspect is the more dynamic one.[25]

PORTABLE CANADIAN
HERO 2, 1935
1972
graphite pencil on paper
213.4 x 335.3 cm
plate 22

1 Dick Harrison, *Unnamed Country*, (Edmonton: University of Alberta Press, 1977), p. 1.

2 Personal interview with Norman Yates, 12 December 1980.

3 George Melnyk, "For an Independent Hairy Hill: The Populist Art of the West," p. 17.

4 Personal interview with Norman Yates, 12 December 1980.

5 George Melnyk, "For an Independent Hairy Hill," p. 17.

6 Jim Simpson, "Masterful drawings by city artist," *Edmonton Journal,* 30 March 1973, TAB9.

7 The economic depression, combined with severe drought conditions, had a serious impact on the prairie economy which was largely based on agriculture in the 1930s. Many farmers lost their land to the "impersonal" eastern banks. Furthermore, the social tradition of the extended farming family was often disrupted as young men left the land to look for work elsewhere.

8 George Melnyk, "From the People - From the Land - The Art of Norman Yates," *Vie des Arts,* 22 (Autumn, 1977), English translation, p. 90.

9 Ibid., p. 21.

10 George Melnyk, "For an Independent Hairy Hill," p. 17. The author quotes from a televised statement made by Norman Yates in 1974.

11 Questionnaire for Alberta Culture. Visual Arts Branch, 1972, p. 7.

12 See "Prairie Spaces and Places," *Artscanada,* 29, no. 169/170/171 (Autumn, 1972).

13 Personal interview with Norman Yates, 12 December 1980.

14 Jim Simpson, TAB 9.

15 Norman Yates, "Landscape into Landscape," *Norman Yates Drawings and Paintings,* introduction by Raymond Ouellet (Edmonton Art Gallery, 1976).

16 See Edmund Husserl, *The Function of the Sciences and the Meaning of Man,* trans. and intro. by Paul Piccone and James E. Hansen (Evanston: Northwestern University Press, 1972) pp.61–86.

17 Maurice Merleau-Ponty, *The Primacy of Perception,* ed. John Wild (Evanston: Northwestern University Studies in Phenomenology and Existential Philosophy, 1964), p. xvi.

18 Personal interview with Norman Yates, 4 February 1981.

19 Ibid.

20 Ibid.

21 Yates, Questionnaire for Alberta Culture, p.7.

22 Guy Robert, *Lemieux.* Trans. John David Allan. (Toronto: Gage Publishing, 1975), p. 178.

23 Yates, "Landscape into Landscape."

24 Yates, "Filmwest in the West," p. 88.

25 Personal interview with Norman Yates, 4 February 1981.

1975 marks another important turning point in Norman Yates' career, for it was in that year that he held his first *Landspace* exhibition.[1] Since then, in all of his exhibited work, this prairie painter has transformed his personal perceptions of the Alberta landscape, or landspace as he has come to call the particularly spacious land, into an original artistic statement. This body of work consists of mixed media drawings on paper, called *Land Drawings,* and paintings done in acrylic on canvas, the *Landspace Paintings.*

The *Land Drawings* are usually smaller works which Yates completes in one session out of doors. He works rapidly as he feels that he can "get to his vision quickly" in this way.[2] While manipulating the various media, usually charcoal, graphite, and acrylic, he attempts to transfer his immediate perceptions of the environment onto the surface of the two-dimensional paper. Included in his immediate perception of a space is what Yates believes to be a dynamic relationship between himself and the space he has entered. It is this relationship that he attempts to capture in his portrayal of the space surrounding his body in these rapidly executed drawings.

However, with the large *Landspace Paintings,* Yates attempts to "deal with the full spatial possibilities" of the land and the sky.[3] Along with the dynamic relationship between the artist and the space which begins as he enters the landscape, he feels that, as he perceives a space and understands it, his own response to it changes. In a theoretical sense, his changing perceptions of the space cause aspects of the actual space to appear changed.[4] Yates attempts, then, in the large paintings to capture more than the immediate nature of the relationship between the painter and the landscape. He also attempts to capture the relationship between himself and the space through time.

Furthermore, Yates explains that he attempts to depict

what he calls a "more spherical relationship, a broader relationship."[5]

Another element for me is all of those forces that have occurred out of my control. I am aware of my perceptions of space and the space which affects my perceptions. But I have a feeling that surrounding me and constantly influencing me and itself constantly being influenced by my existence in it, there is in effect the space that is behind me. Both the time elements that have gone into the making of the existing space and the existence of the source of light that is itself constantly changing, force an awareness on me that I am only part of the whole system rather than the central part.... It is this third broad series of events that go on all the time, that are effective on both my perceptions and space.[6]

This third element mentioned by Yates, the space-time continuum in which all things exist, may be perceived while viewing a *Landspace* painting. The image tends to expand beyond the canvas in all directions, suggesting the space that exists beyond the painter's perceptions. So, from a starting point of his perception of the space surrounding his body, Yates brings all of his experience and knowledge to bear in creating a work pertaining to *Landspace,* as he attempts to capture not only the essence of the Alberta landscape, but the relationship between man and the prairie, and a universal image of space.

Yates simply differentiates these *Landspace* drawings and paintings by number, indicating the continuing, serial nature of his work as it develops over time. This practice also leads the viewer away from attempting to recognize specific geographic locations in the works or in giving the works an overly symbolic interpretation; instead it guides the viewer to become perceptually engaged with the spatial aspects of the drawings and paintings.

In *Two Space with Figures No. 3,* 1975 (plate 24), Yates continues his ongoing interest of relating the human figure to its environment. Here, the artist attempts to relate the figures from the *Survival Series* to the prairie landscape of his Land Studio both structurally and symbolically.

In an attempt to depict his perceptions of the environment, Yates divides the landscape into bands which appear on the paper as surface oriented areas. Thus, without descriptive detail, he attempts to translate his perception of the landscape into a surface energy across the pictorial space. While the land is full of surface texture and colour, the white band containing the figures is isolated by the absence of colour and by the realistic figures rendered in diminished size.

In painting, the relationship of figures to landscape traditionally tells the viewer something about the artist's attitude toward man's place in the universe. Yates explains that by including recognizable shapes of people in his abstracts, he has found a way of portraying the close relationship between humans and the harsh environment they struggle to subdue. The figures are in the landscape, yet are separate from it and not part of that landscape. At the same time, an artist's treatment of the human figure tells the viewer something about the artist's attitude toward humanity, including himself. Yates believes that the artist and figure relate immediately because their shared humanness creates a spatial tension between the two.

In spite of my feeling that the figure was out of context, not fully related, the figure was still nevertheless a reflection of myself. I was the other person watching

that figure in space, watching the figure as that figure was watching me. It's a kind of mirror, a sensitive mirror.[7]

The belief that the world is a 'mirror' is shared by Merleau-Ponty, who explains his belief in this way:

The enigma is that my body simultaneously sees and is seen. That which looks at all things can also look at itself and recognize, in what it sees, the 'other side' of its power of looking. It sees itself seeing; it touches itself touching; it is visible and sensitive for itself.[8]

Like Lemieux's *Self Portrait* of 1974, in which the artist includes anonymous figures from previous paintings, Yates explores the meaning of his own humanity, and his relationship to others and to land in *Two Space with Figures No. 3.*

With *Landspace Two,* 1975 (plate 25), Yates begins to struggle with what Illingworth Kerr calls a "domineering tyrant," the prairie horizon.[9] On the open prairie, where one can see clearly for long distances in all directions, the demarcation between land and sky forms a circle around the viewer, with the centre of the circle at the spot where the viewer is standing. The horizon that appears to the viewer as a line separating earth and sky exists for all to see and so exists in each perceiver's mind. Perceiving the horizon as a circle around his body, Yates is aware that the total horizon cannot be perceived at one glance:

The horizon exists in my mind beyond my simple perception. My awareness of it is that it actually goes beyond my perception. Even when I put a line on the paper, it is the equivalent of the horizon, but only part of it. I can only grasp a bit of it.[10]

The circle of the horizon is not static, but changes as the viewer's position changes. Merleau-Ponty explained the principle of creating new space surrounding oneself by changing one's position on the earth:

Immersed in the visible by his body, itself visible, the see-er does not appropriate what he sees; he merely approaches it by looking, he opens himself to the world...I say of a thing that it is moved; but my body moves itself; it is not blind for itself, it radiates from a self.[11]

As Yates attempted to come to a creative interpretation of his experience in the space of the prairie, a line on the canvas became the horizon, in his mind. When the artist moves around the canvas, flat on the ground of the Land Studio, he changes the line or adds lines to relate to his actual response to the new horizon that his movement has created.

With the experimental *Landspace Two,* Yates again breaks the landscape up into geometric colour areas. Above a primary horizon line of varied thickness is a spacious, neutral, horizontally oriented zone. Below this horizon is a contrasting active area consisting of orange and blue colour areas which vaguely refer to land and sky. However, here colour is used largely for its own sake, unsubordinated to description. For instance, in the central square plane, the blue-orange dynamic is most active as the blue splashes of colour vibrate to the surface. The neutral colour of the sky reappears in the land area to add cohesion to the work; a practice of uniting the various areas of the canvas with colour that Yates often employs in the *Landspace* works. In this way, the blue area below the primary horizon represents an illusion of space or sky and acts as a counterpoint to the grey in the upper band. The disposition of the warm yellow and orange tones acts in a similar manner to create an illusion of

TWO SPACE WITH FIGURES NO. 3
1975
acrylic and graphite pencil on paper
66.0 x 101.5 cm
plate 24

LANDSPACE TWO
1975
acrylic on canvas
127.0 x 203.2 cm
plate 25

the spacious land. With more than one viewpoint and several planes of colour, Yates seems to attempt to make the perceptual phenomena compatible with formal visual forces on the surface of the canvas, a method which results in a very personal abstraction of the space.

The next painting to be considered, *Landspace Sixteen,* 1975 (plate 26), is a horizontally oriented work of great scale. While Yates painted at one end of the canvas, he could hardly see the other end and so he was forced to attempt to maintain the whole concept in his mind. However, as the surface changed through the process of creation, the painter found that he constantly changed his concept as he worked.

In this painting, Yates directly attacks that "domineering tyrant" the horizon — the relationship between reality and illusion — by joining three separate canvases. Here, the literal divisons become horizons for Yates. Conceptually, this was an important test for the painter, to leave the physical divisions as they are and yet suggest that one is to perceive them pictorially as horizons. He felt that if he could accomplish this feat, a dynamic relationship between the literal separations of the canvases and the illusion of what the divisions visually suggest could add energy and life to the painting.

Landspace Sixteen is a large acrylic painting consisting of a series of applications of hues made by keeping the canvas soaking wet during the process of creation. The arcs of light consist of layers of thin glazes. With an overall, unifying quality of smoothly handled paint, Yates attempts, by means of colour, to create two spatial areas surrounding the centre of the canvas. The orange used in these spatial areas relates to the central orange band, unifying the work through these colour correspondences. The light arcs are also meant to be perceived as suggestions of movement so that the spatial areas, perceived as either land or sky, may appear to rotate around the fixed centre representing the land.

Barely discernable in the centre of the painting are two shadowy figures which are part of Yates' ongoing interest in exploring the relationship between man and his environment. As Laurence Ricou asserts in his study of prairie literature, *Vertical Man/Horizontal World*, "the landscape, and man's relation to it, is the concrete situation with which the prairie artist initiates his re-creation of the human experience."[12] Yates, who has been interested in humanity throughout his career, likewise attempts to explore in his work man's relationship to the space he occupies. The figures in *Landspace Sixteen* were drawn in pencil directly on the raw canvas before any paint was applied. Through the physical process of applying the paint, the figures became more and more submerged. In this way, Yates hoped to retain the figures in the landscape as part of the space and yet isolate them from that space with colour. However, colour and light force the submerged figures to the surface, creating a tension within the work which several critics have found vaguely disconcerting.[13] These figures appear small and insignificant, as is usually the case when Yates includes figures in a *Landspace* painting. The painter discusses this aspect of the figures and reveals his basic belief in the superior strength of nature:

The small people have a slightly helpless quality that accounts for the scale of the figures and their slightly isolated, lost-looking quality. They're always standing there wondering what to do. Nature always knows what to do, but mankind is not that fortunate.... The inclusion of the figure is much more visually inclined to what's actually happening in the landscape. When I look at my own drawings, the figures take on more symbolic significance as figures of loneliness or conflict or the grouping of them for protection. Then that cycle

affects the next set of drawings or paintings; but it really started as a visual occurrence.[14]

With *Landspace Seventeen,* 1976 (plate 27), Yates again creates a painting with three separate canvases in order to render his perceptions of the dynamics of open space. The overall horizontal quality of the work is reinforced by the divisions between the canvases. The relationship between the different canvases creates illusions of horizons, in much the same way as does the relationship between the earth and sky in the actual landscape. In this way, the two horizons separate three areas that can all be perceived equally as land or sky.

To Yates, the spacious, horizontal prairie is an image of freedom:

I have almost a recurring vision, partially a dream of sitting on the prairie. I did that mostly as a child as I lived on the outskirts of a town and in five minutes I could be on the open prairie. I can remember and feel strongly about the openness of the prairie, never being enclosed.[15]

Landspace Thirty-Nine, 1979 (plate 30), is a painting which Yates completed between two series of works and can be seen as an introduction to his most recent work. Here, with an illusion of a storm cloud on the horizon, Yates allows more expression and distortion of his actual visual perceptions to occur. The cycle between illusion, expression, and abstraction has been a constantly recurring characteristic of his work throughout his career and continues into the present time. In spite of the fact that this work introduces a return to a greater interest in 'expression,' the painter continues to match theory to the manifestation of the surface.

In *Landspace Thirty-Nine* one can recognize the initiation of a more subdued palette, combined with

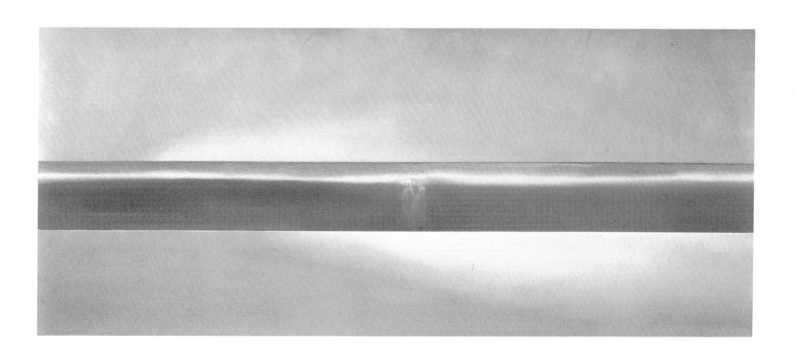

LANDSPACE SIXTEEN
1975
acrylic on canvas
115.0 x 275.0 cm
plate 26

LANDSPACE SEVENTEEN
1976
acrylic on canvas
125.0 x 275.0 cm
plate 27

LANDSPACE TWENTY
1976
acrylic on canvas
112.0 x 275.0 cm
plate 28

the appearance of an overall uniform texture which at times seems to transform the pictorial into the tactile qualities of a finely woven tapestry. The artist recognizes that seeing his wife, weaver Whynona Yates, create her works has given him an even greater appreciation for the texture, surface, colour and scale of woven fabric which he feels has influenced his ideas on these aspects of his own work.[16]

Structurally, the dark, blurred shape at the right appears to press forward toward the surface. The sharply drawn line receding from the lower left corner of the canvas to the horizon at the right suggests a road diminishing into the distance. The perspective illusion of the road forces one to perceive the ominous dark object in the distant prairie space. Yates says, "the exaggerated sky formations occur but never to this intensity, except perhaps in our memory."[17] The use of his memory of his sensate experiences of the prairie in addition to painting the scene 'on the spot' is further evident in his own words:

Everytime I make one of these paintings it's certainly related to my past experiences in the country. I always have a tremendous sense of déjà vu, a new cycling of a vision that I'd had before, especially in spatial terms.... In Saskatchewan we used to get that 'build up' on the horizon. It's a slightly ominous feeling that prairie people live with.[18]

The cloud ominously presses into the viewer's space and if the viewer has had personal experiences with the prairie, it reawakens his memories and perceptions of that landscape. Yates manipulates the pictorial space in this precise manner in order to stimulate not only the viewer's immediate perception of the work of art, but also his memory as he recalls his own personal associations with the space of the prairie.

Yates continued to produce drawings in this latest series. *Land Drawing No. 13,* 1980 (plate 31), suggests an oriental feeling that Yates' work sometimes evokes. While in Japan, in 1979, he was impressed with the handling of space by past and present Japanese painters. He feels that the contemporary Japanese artists he met were attempting to combine space and surface in their works. Their answer to the dilemma was to compose works emphasizing compositional movements in a two-dimensional direction, extending vertically or horizontally as Yates had also done. He sensed that contemporary Japanese painters were struggling to get some illusion of space in a western sense while retaining their traditional surface, while he, Yates, was struggling in the opposite direction.

In *Land Drawing No. 13,* Yates attempts to achieve an overall spacious illusion using light/dark contrasts so typical of the prairie winter landscape with its stark beauty of leafless trees and snow. The large, dark form on the left contrasts to the small, horizontal shape on the right, enhancing the suggestion of space. The individual strokes add to the illusion evoking an atmospheric winterscape.

The more Yates became imbued with the Alberta landscape, the more he became aware of the light-reflective qualities of snow. He began to believe that it is the snow that partly gives a prairie dweller his sense of place and affects one's perception of space while living in Alberta. Here he attempts to capture the great contrasts that can appear in the winter landscape when a dark area comes directly into contact with a brightly lit area. He feels that often these dark/light contrasts in the winter landscape of the prairie add to one's visual sense of place.

The latest *Landspace Series* ends with *Landspace 50,* 1980 (plate 32). With this large work, Yates attempts to retain the structural notion that the division between the canvases equals the perceived horizons. Further, he wants to combine this concept with illusionary

LANDSPACE TWENTY-FIVE
1976
acrylic on canvas
107.0 x 275.0 cm
plate 29

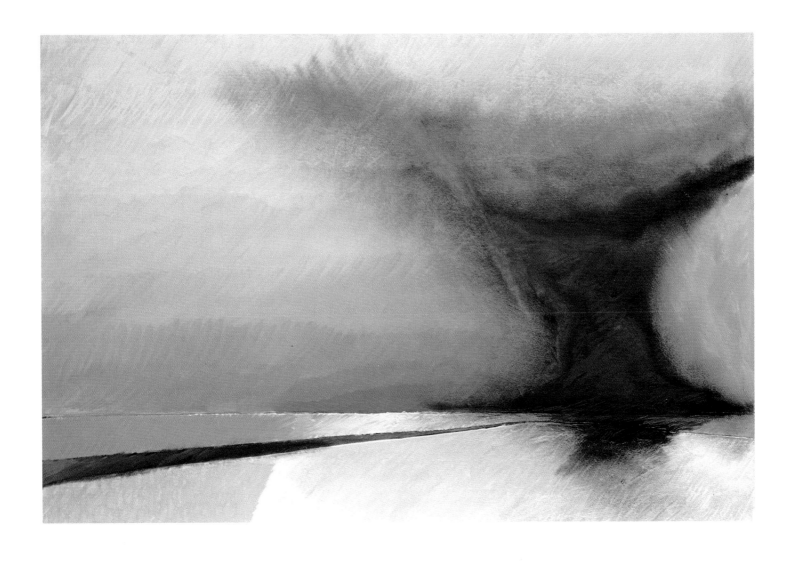

LANDSPACE THIRTY-NINE
1979
acrylic on canvas
81.5 x 122.0 cm
plate 30
opposite

LAND DRAWING 13
1980
charcoal colour, graphite on
paper
56.0 x 76.0 cm
plate 31

LANDSPACE FIFTY
1980
acrylic on canvas
229.0 x 550.0 cm
plate 32

horizons painted onto the surface. The horizon to which the viewer relates as a symbolic demarcation between land and sky is also intended by the painter. Along with these ideas, he attempts to provide the viewer with a vision of the prairie in front of which the viewer will remember his personal perceptual experiences of the region. In this work, many horizons separate areas of colour; at times, the light and dark colour areas interact directly, while at other times, the artist uses a gradual shift in colour as well as light. In using these visual forces, the painter attempts to portray the essence of the prairie through time including multiple cycles of time and space.

In the following passage, Yates sums up his current perceptions of the 'landscape' which he has studied for so long:

When I'm in the landscape, I have always a strong awareness of all the elements going on . . . of the inevitability of that process which is something I enjoy. Because unlike that vertical figure on the horizontal world from my paintings, I feel much more a part of it and I'm not so anxious about being isolated from it because I know that one day, I too will become horizontal and simply a part of the universal fact. So it's a slightly more humble position, but equally a more realistic one in some ways. It's not so tight a relationship. It permits an expansion of perception yet a very close one-to-one intimacy with the process of nature.[19]

1 At Latitude 53 Gallery, Edmonton, September 30–October 18, 1975.

2 Personal interview with Norman Yates, 4 February 1981.

3 Ibid.

4 Ibid.

5 Ibid.

6 Ibid.

7 Ibid.

8 Merleau-Ponty, p. 162.

9 Illingworth Kerr, in an interview with Bente Roed-Cochran for "Alberta: Concerning the History of the Visual Arts," *Visual Arts Newsletter*, 3, No. 1 (Winter, 1981), 15.

10 Personal interview with Norman Yates, 4 February 1981.

11 Merleau-Ponty, p. 162.

12 Laurence Ricou, *Vertical Man/Horizontal World* (Vancouver: University of British Columbia Press, 1973), p. xi.

13 See Marytka Kosinski, "Identity Found in Western Landscape," *Edmonton Journal*, 4 December 1976, p. 37.

14 Personal interview with Norman Yates, 4 February 1981.

15 Ibid.

16 Critics have commented upon the woven appearance of Yates' recent work. See Mary Grayson, "Yates in his Maturity Creates Magic," *Edmonton Journal*, 25 October 1980, p. C9.

17 Personal interview with Norman Yates, 4 February 1981.

18 Ibid.

19 Ibid.

In 1972, a dramatic change occurred in Norman Yates' work. Throughout his career, he has constantly searched for an artistic expression that would have strength in the honesty of its origin in his personal convictions about life and art. Most importantly, he has always wished to communicate to his fellow humans in a meaningful way. From his early realistic figurative paintings which involved some distortion for compositional and expressive purposes, the artist has continually explored the relationship between the human figure, representing all humanity, and its environment by utilizing varying degrees of abstraction and symbolism expressed in various media. These explorations reached their peak in the years between 1970 and 1972 when Yates devoted himself to experiments with various electronic media to the total exclusion of drawing and painting. Although these new activities were interesting and exciting, Yates did not feel that they gave him the means to truly express his artistic and personal concepts developed during the 1950s and the 1960s. Finally, however, in 1972, Yates combined a medium, style, and subject which brought about the consolidation of his artistic endeavors and his emergence as an important Alberta landscape painter.

Integral to Yates' maturity as an artist was his return to what he calls the tradition and purity of drawing and painting. Working within this artistic tradition, which stems from his personal roots—his childhood interests and his formal training—he now feels most comfortable. Yates continues his concern of relating the spatial qualities which he perceives in the physical world to the humans who inhabit that space, but now restricts himself to transforming these visual perceptions onto the two-dimensional paper or canvas. At the same time, the environment that he attempts to portray is his own home, the western prairie.

This important aspect in Yates' work coincided with the belief of several Alberta artists and writers in the validity of an artistic expression inspired by their own perceptions of their local roots. Yates' own emergence as an Alberta landscape painter was strongly influenced most obviously by his participation in the "For an Independent Hairy Hill" exhibition, his relationship with the Alberta literary circle associated with the *White Pelican* magazine, and especially his friendship with Wilfred Watson.

With renewed energy and conviction, Yates made great advances in 1972 with his early attempts to portray the prairies. In *Four Space Elevator with Brand* and the *Regina Riot Series,* he combined his past and present visual perceptions of the space of the prairie with western history. In these attempts to depict the vast space of the West, the artist divided the perceived space in various ways and used silhouette drawing, leaving large areas of white paper untouched.

Possibly the greatest influence on Yates' emergence as a prairie landscape painter of originality and strength occurred in 1972 with the beginning of his direct and continual relationship with his Land Studio. It was his visual perception of this land near Edmonton that led Yates to think of his surroundings as landspace. He discusses the importance of the great sense of space one receives on the vast, boundless prairie as a "vision" leading to a "feeling" he has about the prairie in the following quotation:

My experience on the land gives me ... a notion of space, that is a vision of an expanse of country combined with a feeling of continuous and unbounded extension in every direction — landspace.[1]

The resulting *Quarter Section Series* of 1972 which was executed with great simplicity on Yates' new Land Studio, clearly places the artist in the western Canadian tradition of landscape painters who attempt to translate their visual perceptions of the vast space, made

apparent by the flat expanse of land, bright light, and prairie colour, into a visual art. Since this new impetus in his career, Yates' mature work, consisting of the *Land Drawings* and *Landspace Paintings* carried out between 1975 and the present, exhibit consistency in style and content. These drawings and paintings reflect the artist's awareness of aspects of modern art of the second half of the twentieth century originating in the post-war New York School and now so pervasive throughout the world. The works also reflect his previous explorations into spatial concepts using various media such as stage design, holography, photography, and filmmaking. So, contrary to the 'searching years' prior to 1972, one finds that Yates has been able to consolidate all of his artistic and personal beliefs into his personal imagery in the *Landspace Series.*

A closer analysis of the formal characteristics of the artist's *Landspace* drawings and paintings indicates the fusion of the formal concerns with which he had long been working and his visual perceptions of the space of the prairie. An overall stability within the pictorial space is often maintained through the use of a classically balanced composition based on opposing horizontal, vertical, or circular movements of force. The size and shape of the paper or canvas is always carefully chosen to add to the compositional dynamics of the total work. At times, he extends the composition over two or more canvases which are related in a vertical or horizontal format, often extending the repetitive, serial manipulation of these compositional characteristics with each brush stroke. This overall stability, so evident in the mature drawings and paintings, leads the viewer to perceive the timeless stability of the prairie space, as it flows into infinity, extending by suggestion beyond the confines of the paper or canvas.

The interrelationship of opposing forces can be found throughout Yates' oeuvre in the use of colour stemming

73

from the theories of Josef Albers and the use of visual contrasts rooted in the theories of Hans Hofmann. Likewise, the importance of variety in the handling of the paint has always intrigued Yates. This method of relating or juxtaposing various formal aspects of a drawing or painting to set up dynamic relationships is always fused with the subject matter or theme of the work. From an early notion of a simple contrast of painterly qualities to reinforce his theme, as seen in the early school works like *The Gate,* his use of opposites evolved slowly, until the 1970s when a more mature dialectical expression of the complex relationship between opposites was achieved.

Furthermore, close attention to the process of creating a work of art, coupled with the explorations into various media has ultimately added richness to Yates' work. The use of several modules created separately and brought together forming one total image, or a large horizontal pictorial space which cannot be taken in at a single glance by the painter as he works, indicates the importance which Yates places on time, experimentation, and process expressed in form and content. By concentrating on the process in this way, he attempts to integrate the space and time dynamics of the process so that they become part of the spatial dynamics of the work of art.

These structural and stylistic characteristics of Yates' drawings and paintings, exhibiting the use of dynamic opposites, have always been inspired by the artist's perceptions of natural phenomena. In Yates' mature work, the use of these relationships to compose a painting now stems from his perceptions of the prairie space in particular and has led him away from arriving at a composition based on the interrelationships between tangible objects. Now, he instead attempts to capture the dynamics of an intangible, flexible space determined by his own visual perceptions of that space.

Attempting to capture this elusive space of the prairie can only be achieved after a sensitive visual relationship with the land and the sky is established. Yates' perception of the horizon, and his belief that it is the light that defines the spaciousness of the prairie, form the basis of his renditions of the 'landspace.'

Another essential ingredient in the *Landspace* works is Yates' insistence on the value of what he calls "the mark on the surface" unsubordinated to description. The importance that he places on the artist's 'touch' has remained a constant concern through the years. He believes it is the human 'touch' that is the most important aspect of a drawing or a painting and gives the work its quality. He further believes that it is this touch by a human artist evident in the least mark on the surface that ultimately gives the work of art its power to communicate, since the viewer recognizes, in the personal mark on the surface, humanity that he shares with the artist. This belief is further supported by Yates' concept that the maintenance of the 'sense of surface' of the pictorial space is an important contemporary tradition that he wishes to explore. Finally, an attempt by Yates to create an art not only of visual interest, but also of tactile, emotional, and intellectual interest gives the viewer more of an awareness of the three-dimensional space of the prairie on the paper or canvas.

Simple geometric forms, already found in Yates' early work, are now a predominant element in his compositions. The horizontal line or division representing the convergence of the flat prairie and the large expanse of sky establishes the basis of the composition. This 'line' reflecting the artist's perception of the prairie defines the work formally and thematically as a landspace, stretching out equally in all directions from the perceiver. At the same time, vertical lines, divisions, or actual figures represent the artist and thus all of humanity, because Yates believes that we all share in our visual relationship to the space surrounding our bodies.

Structurally and thematically, then, Yates' longstanding interest in his fellow man has led him to an exploration of the relationship between the human figure and its environment and the translation of that relationship on to the pictorial space. In the words of George Melnyk, "Man and the land are the two poles of Norman Yates' art. His creative space is the tenuous balance between man and the land."[2]

Related to the artist's perceptions of his surroundings, extending to include humanity, is Yates' concern with the relationship between the viewer standing in his space and the pictorial space culminating in an attempt to lead the viewer to enter into a dynamic perceptual relationship with the drawing or painting. In the early *Landspace* works, figures are included by the artist to represent all humanity, including the artist and observer. When the viewer in his space perceives the figures in the pictorial space, it is hoped by the artist that the viewer will relate to the figures as if he is seeing himself in a sensitive mirror. However, in the late works, the figure has become fused with the artist/observer.

With great harmony between style and content, Yates' translation of his personal perceptions of the prairie landscape reaches out to the viewer in his space, leading the viewer to a more sensitive awareness of his relationship to the surrounding world. As is often the case in the mature work of one who has achieved an important artistic expression, Yates' *Landspace Series* is marked by simplicity, assurance, strength and clarity.

Yates sums up his feelings about the role of the artist and art in the following passage:

An artist's visual perception is a tiny touch of understanding that comes about in the manner of a contribution to a whole set of understandings. If artists are totally involved, to whatever degree of sophistication, they contribute to a little bit of our understanding. When that is added to the total understanding, it can be very significant.... Most artists I have liked are part of the understanding of the whole. If you can just offer (a contribution to society) before it's too late.... That's philosophically my feeling about art. The true motivation for an artist has to be a contribution.[3]

1 Yates, "Landscape into Landspace."

2 George Melnyk, "Painter of Land and Light," in *Norman Yates: Drawings and Paintings*

3 Personal interview with Norman Yates, 4 February 1981.

Harper, J. Russell. *Painting in Canada: A History.* Toronto: University of Toronto Press, 1966.

Harrison, Dick. *Unnamed Country: The Struggle for a Canadian Prairie Fiction.* Edmonton: University of Alberta Press, 1977.

Husserl, Edmond. *The Function of the Sciences and the Meaning of Man.* Trans. and Intro. Paul Piccone and James E. Hansen. Evanston: Northwestern University Press, 1972.

Kosinski, Marytka L. "Time of Transition, Contradictions." *Edmonton Journal,* 18 October 1975, p. 75.
"Identity Found in Western Landscape." *Edmonton Journal,* 4 December 1976, p. 37.

Melnyk, George. "For an Independent Hairy Hill: The Populist Art of the West." *White Pelican,* 5, No. 1 (1975): 14–25.
"The Art of Norman Yates: From the People, From the Land." *Vies des Arts,* 22, No. 49–51 (Autumn, 1977): 90–91.
"Norman Yates Painter of Land and Light." In *Norman Yates Drawings and Paintings.* Intro. Raymond Ouellet. Edmonton: The Edmonton Art Gallery, 1976.

McLuhan, Marshall. *Understanding Media: The Extensions of Man.* New York: McGraw-Hill, 1964.

Merleau-Ponty, Maurice. *Phenomenology and Perception.* Trans. Colin Smith. New York: The Humanities Press, 1962.
The Primacy of Perception. Ed. John Wild. Evanston: Northwestern University Press, 1964.

Reid, Dennis. *A Concise History of Canadian Painting.* Toronto: Oxford University Press, 1973.

Ricou, Laurence R. *Vertical Man/Horizontal World: Man and Landscape in Canadian Prairie Fiction.* Vancouver: University of British Columbia Press, 1973.

"Circumference of Absence: Land and Space in the Poetry of the Canadian Plains." In *Canadian Plains Studies 6.* Ed. Richard Allen. Regina: University of Regina, 1976. pp.66–76.

Rockman, Arnold. "How 20 Canadians Draw the Line." *Canadian Art,* 21, No. 90: 85–95.

Robert, Guy. *Lemieux.* Trans. John David Allan. Toronto: Gage Publishing, 1975.

Simpson, Jim. "Masterful Drawings by City Artist." *Edmonton Journal,* 30 March 1973, p. TAB9.

Storm, Hyemeyohsts. *Seven Arrows.* New York, 1973.

Thomson, Hugh. "Tandem Bike Artist Exhibits at Beaches." *Toronto Daily Star,* 11 November 1952, p. 7.

Unknown. "Artists Told to Express Emotions." *Edmonton Journal,* 11 February 1961, p. 26.

"Yates Opens Exhibit at Art Gallery." *Edmonton Journal,* 24 March 1973, p. 69.

Yates, Norman. "Four Edmonton Artists." *Artscanada,* 26, No. 128/139 (October, 1969): 42–43.

"Extensions." December 1969, from artist's personal files.

Designing Clytemnestra, CKUA January 1970, from artist's personal files.

"Art Becomes an Elastic Mosaic." *The Gateway,* 27 February 1970, p. C5.

"Filmmakers in Edmonton: An Interim Report." *Artscanada,* 27, No. 141/142 (April, 1970): 46–48.

"Environment '70 in Alberta." *Artscanada,* 27 No. 146/147 (August, 1970): 60–61.

Questionnaire for Alberta Culture. Visual Arts Branch, 1972, from artist's personal files, pp. 1–7.

"Filmwest in the West." *Artscanada,* No. 169/170/171 (Autumn, 1972): 88–93.

"Metal Flags and Cloth Medals." *Edge,* No. 9 (Summer, 1980): 77–78.

"Toward the Full Moon." *Interface,* 3, No. 5 (Summer, 1980): 80–83.

"Working Description of the Library Mural." from artist's personal files.

1923   September 7: Edward Norman Yates born to Albert M. and Maude Yates in Calgary, Alberta.

1924–1940   Family moves to Regina, Saskatchewan. Attends Herchmer Public School and Scott Collegiate Institute. Publishes cartoons in the high school newsletter.

1941   Joins the RCAF and studies electronics in Montreal through the Air Force Program.

1942–1946   Stationed in England as a radar technician. Occasionally joins life drawing classes for Air Force people held at a nearby Art School. Makes decision to become an artist.

1945   Marries Whynona Humphreys.

1947   Returns to Canada and enrols in Commercial Art course at the Ontario College of Art through the War Veterans Program.

1948   Switches from Commercial Art course to Fine Arts Program, studying painting and graphics. Teachers included Harley Parker, Fred Hagen, Will Ogilvy, Eric Freifield, Jock Macdonald, George Pepper, and G. Röling.

1949   Wins student prize, Ontario College of Art.

1950   Graduates from OCA with first class honours. Travels to England where he works as a bookkeeper for six months. Travels through Northern Europe for three months visiting art galleries and museums.

1951–1953   Returns to Toronto. Work consists mostly of descriptive renditions of people and places that attract him; technique steadily improves.

1954   Accepts a teaching position in the Faculty of Education at the University of Alberta, Edmonton, for one year.

1955   Joins the Fine Arts Department at the University of Alberta. Colleagues include H. G. Glyde and J. B. Taylor. Becomes involved in set and costume design for Studio Theatre.

1956   Accepts permanent appointment with the Fine Arts Department. Meets Wilfred Watson.

1961–1965   *Allegoria Series.*

1961–1962   Alberta representative in the Canadian Society for Education through Art.

1962   Meets Victor Pasmore at the University of Durham, Kings College, Newcastle-on-Tyne.

1963   Returns to Edmonton. Experiments with photography, filmmaking, holography, mixed media constructions, stage design and painting.

1964   Begins term as director of the Fine Arts Gallery, University of Alberta.

1965   Visiting professor at University of British Columbia for summer session. Begins *Throne Room Series.*

1965–1967   University of Alberta representative on the Western Canada Art Circuit. Finishes term as director of Fine Arts Gallery.

1967–1969   Wins Canada Council Senior Arts Award. Last of the *Throne Room Series.*

1970–1976   Art and co-editor of *White Pelican*.

1970–1971   Executive Council of the University Art Association of Canada.

1972   Exhibits in "For an Independent Hairy Hill," a National Gallery of Canada travelling exhibition.

1972–1973   University of Alberta representative, Canadian Artists Representation, Edmonton.

1973   Visiting professor at the University of British Columbia: summer session.

1973–1974   Board of Governors: Canadian Conference of the Arts.

1973–1975   Board Member of the Alberta Art Foundation.

1974   Visiting professor at the University of British Columbia: summer session.

1975–present   *Landspace Series*.

1975   Canada Council Senior Arts Award. Chairman, University of Alberta National Award Committee for Painting and Related Arts.

1976–1978   Chairman, Alberta Art Foundation.

1977   25th Anniversary Queen's Medal. Teaches at Banff School of Fine Arts.

1978   Commendation in appreciation for dedicated and valuable service from the government of Alberta.

1979   Represents the Alberta Art Foundation in arranging a travelling exhibition of Japan. Alberta Achievement Award for excellence in art.

1980   Service Award from the University of Alberta. Visiting artist; Art Summer '80, Charlottetown, PEI.

1981–82   Study Leave Research Grant.

1983   Solo Exhibition, Graphica Art Gallery, Edmonton.

Sizes given represent paper size or canvas size, height before width.

*denotes works included both in the catalogue and the exhibition.

**denotes works represented only in the catalogue.

No asterisk denotes works included only in the exhibition.

Self Portrait*
1950
oil on canvas
60.3 x 60.1 cm
collection of the artist
plate 1

The Gate*
1950
lithograph
33.6 x 25.7 cm
collection of the artist
plate 2

Boat Yard, Toronto
1950
watercolour on paper
45.5 x 61.0 cm
collection of the artist

Study for Girl Drying Her Hair
1953
conte on paper
56.5 x 45.2 cm
collection of the artist

Girl Drying Her Hair*
1954
oil on canvas
82.5 x 61.0 cm
collection of Professor
Maurice J. Boote, Ontario
plate 3

Merry-Go-Round*
1954
watercolour on paper
42.2 x 56.9 cm
collection of the artist
plate 4

Winter Landscape*
1958
ink and gouache on paper
44.8 x 62.6 cm
collection of the artist
plate 5

Two Figures in a Space*
1960
watercolour and pencil on paper
44.7 x 57.0 cm
collection of the artist
plate 6

Allegoria 8*
1961
blue pencil on paper
45.7 x 61.7 cm
collection of The National Gallery of Canada
plate 8

Reclining Nude
1962
oil on board
73.7 x 104.3 cm
collection of Wilfred and Sheila Watson, British Columbia

Allegoria 14*
1963
blue pencil on paper
48.4 x 61.0 cm
collection of Diane E. Bessai, Edmonton
plate 9

Landscape**
1963
gouache on paper
66.8 x 52.0 cm
collection of the artist
plate 10

Durham Landscape**
1963
watercolour and pencil on paper
44.5 x 56.9 cm
collection of the artist
plate 11

North East Village, England
1963
gouache on paper
44.4 x 57.0 cm
collection of the artist

New Town
1963
watercolour and pencil on paper
66.7 x 51.8 cm
collection of the artist

Allegoria 12*
1964
pencil on paper
48.3 x 61.0 cm
collection of the artist
plate 7

Queen Head*
1965
graphite on paper
61.0 x 45.5 cm
collection of the artist
plate 12

Courtesan*
1965
graphite, watercolour, balsa wood, black tape on paper
68.9 x 92.5 cm
collection of the artist
plate 13

Wall Painting I**
1968
acrylic on canvas
101.2 x 101.2 cm
whereabouts unknown
plate 14

Banner Figure
1967
acrylic on canvas
101.1 x 91.7 cm
collection of the artist

Revolving Credit II
1968
acrylic on canvas
121.9 x 121.9 cm
collection of Mary Grayson, Edmonton

Kinetic Foil**
1969
two rows of Alcan aluminum foil
304.8(h) x 243.8(w) x 609.6(d) cm
installation piece, Students' Union Art Gallery, University of Alberta
plate 15

Drawing 2, Regina Riot 1935*
1972
graphite pencil on paper
66.0 x 101.2 cm
collection of The Canada Council, Art Bank, Ottawa
plate 19

Two Space Regina Riot 1935**
1972
graphite pencil on paper
66.0 x 202.4 cm
whereabouts unknown
plate 18

Three Space Regina Riot 1935*
1972
graphite pencil on paper
198.2 x 101.6 cm
collection of the Alberta Art Foundation
plate 20

Four Space Elevator with Brand*
1972
graphite pencil on paper
304.8 x 104.5 cm
collection of the artist
plate 21

Five Space St. Bernard
1972
graphite pencil on paper
266.6 x 113.0 cm
collection of the artist

Quarter Section Sketch
1972
graphite and acrylic on paper
66.0 x 101.2 cm
collection of the artist

Portable Canadian Hero 2, 1935**
1972
graphite pencil on paper
213.4 x 335.3 cm
collection of the artist
plate 22

Two Space Quarter Section No. 20*
1973
acrylic on canvas
167.6 x 304.8 cm
collection of Dr. J. Orrell, Edmonton
plate 23

Quarter Section No. 23**
1974
acrylic on canvas
92.0 x 195.0 cm
collection of the artist
frontispiece

Landspace Two*
1975
acrylic on canvas
127.0 x 203.2 cm
collection of the Government House Foundation, Edmonton
plate 25

Landspace Sixteen*
1975
acrylic on canvas
115.0 x 275.0 cm
collection of Hooke Outdoor Advertising, Calgary
plate 26

Two Space with Figures No. 3*
1975
acrylic and graphite pencil on paper
66.0 x 101.5 cm
collection of the artist
plate 24

Farm Drawing 1
1975
graphite pencil on paper
57.4 x 72.8 cm
collection of the artist

Landspace Seventeen*
1976
acrylic on canvas
125.0 x 275.0 cm
collection of the University of Alberta
plate 27

Landspace Twenty*
1976
acrylic on canvas
112.0 x 275.0 cm
collection of Mr. and Mrs. Sieghard Schmidt, Edmonton
plate 28

Landspace Twenty-one
1976
acrylic on canvas
115.0 x 275.0 cm
on loan from The Simon Fraser Collection, Burnaby, British Columbia

Landspace Twenty-five*
1976
acrylic on canvas
107.0 x 275.0 cm
collection of The Confederation Centre Art Gallery and Museum, P.E.I.
plate 29

Farm Drawing 7
1977
graphite pencil on paper
48.3 x 66.0 cm
private collection

Landspace Thirty-nine*
1979
acrylic on canvas
81.5 x 122.0 cm
collection of Francine Gravel, British Columbia
plate 30

Landspace Forty
1979
acrylic on canvas
90.0 x 190.0 cm
collection of Mr. and Mrs. J. D. Tilston, Calgary

Landspace Forty-one
1979
acrylic on canvas
95.0 x 200.0 cm
collection of the artist

Landspace Forty-four
1980
acrylic on canvas
110.0 x 190.0 cm
collection of the Alberta Art
Foundation, Edmonton

Landspace Fifty**
1980
acrylic on canvas
229.0 x 550.0 cm
collection of Oxford
Development Group,
Edmonton
plate 32

Land Drawing 3
1980
charcoal colour, graphite on
paper
56.0 x 76.0 cm
collection of the artist

Land Drawing 13*
1980
charcoal colour, graphite on
paper
56.0 x 76.0 cm
private collection
plate 31

82

Land Drawing 27
1980
charcoal colour, graphite on
paper
56.0 x 76.0 cm
private collection

Land Drawing 2
1981
charcoal colour, pastel,
graphite on paper
56.0 x 76.0 cm
collection of the artist
courtesy of Graphica
Gallery, Edmonton

Land Drawing 5
1981
charcoal colour, pastel,
graphite on paper
56.0 x 76.0 cm
collection of Garrel Clark,
Edmonton

Land Drawing 10
1981
charcoal colour, pastel,
graphite on paper
77.0 x 108.0 cm
collection of Mary and Peter
Smilanich, Edmonton

Land Drawing 14
1982
charcoal colour, pastel,
graphite on paper
77.0 x 108.0 cm
collection of the Alberta Art
Foundation

Landspace Sixty-five*
1982/83
charcoal colour, pastel,
graphite on paper
232.0 x 288.5 cm
collection of the artist
cover